The Sugar Maple Press Anthology of Nature Poems

The Sugar Maple Press Anthology of Nature Poems

Compilation, Introduction, and Photos by Greg Fox

SUGAR MAPLE PRESS

SUGAR MAPLE PRESS

Sugar Maple Press

www.sugarmaplepress.com

e-mail: sugarmaplepress@yahoo.com

Sugar Maple Press edition: Copyright © 2014 by Greg Fox

All Sugar Maple Press titles are available at special quantity discounts for bulk purchases, for sales promotions, premiums, fundraising, educational or institutional use.
Contact us at sugarmaplepress@yahoo.com for details.

ISBN-13:   978-0615990576
ISBN-10:   0615990576

First Sugar Maple Press Trade Paperback Printing: Spring, 2014

Cover photo: Shaftsbury, Vermont by Greg Fox
Back Cover photo: Arlington, Vermont by Greg Fox

*Dedicated to everyone who's working to
sustain the environment and to
keep this beautiful planet alive & well!*

*And to all of the poets whose work graces this volume…
thank you for sharing your inspiration with the world,
and for helping to make this collection shine!*

Table of Contents

NOTE: All photographs by Greg Fox

Introduction

The beauty of nature never really goes out of style, does it? One cannot relegate the gorgeousness of a cherry blossom tree in full bloom to a certain era. It was breathtaking 1200 years ago, and it's breathtaking today.

Yet, much of nature's beauty can have a fleeting quality. As lovely as that cherry blossom tree may be, bedecked in its myriad of pink flowers, the bloom is short-lived. Within a week or so, all of the petals have fallen.

New England's hills are set ablaze in October with the fiery foliage of sugar maple trees. And while this stunning display lasts a bit longer than the cherry blossoms of Spring, by November, the maple tree branches have begun to bare against the approaching winter skies.

However, as each season fades into the next, new beauties emerge to capture our attention. The cherry blossoms of Spring may be gone, but now the cerulean blue hydrangeas of Summer burst into bloom, accompanied by fluttering orange butterflies and the fragrance of fresh, sweet peaches coming into season. And in Autumn, as the last Maple leaves fall to the ground, delicate snowflakes in their crystalline beauty descend from the heavens to coat everything in a luscious Winter white. (To some, I realize, the snows of winter are anything but "delightful", and hardly "short-lived". But when one looks at the individual snowflake itself... when magnified, a spectacular, hexagonal crystalline structure... each one unique it its own complex design...this is perhaps one of nature's most delicate and short-lived, yet beguilingly gorgeous works of art).

And while these various gifts of each season...the Spring cherry blossoms, the Summer peaches, the Fall foliage, and the Winter snowflakes...may be short-lived...we can all take comfort in the assurance of their return each year to delight us once again with their annual arrival. Provided, of course, that the earth continues to regenerate itself under the duress of so much global industrialization and outpouring of manmade pollutants. Perhaps now, it is more important than ever...for us and for future generations...to refocus our attention on the beauty of the natural world. If something is treasured, it is more likely to be cared for and cultivated healthily. And the earth is in deep need of that sort of care right now. That the beauty of nature and the changing seasons may continue on for millenia to come.

The language of poetry is particularly suited to capture the beauty of nature. And the poems within this volume, collected from various poets over the last several centuries, all reflect on, examine, and respond to the natural world, as relevant today as when they were first written. And I hope that my photographs within this volume help to capture a bit of that natural beauty, too.

Enjoy!

Greg Fox
Northport, New York
3/13/2014

Poems of Spring

Spring

Henry Wadsworth Longfellow

Gentle Spring! - in sunshine clad,
Well dost thou thy power display!
For Winter maketh the light heart sad,
And thou, - thou makest the sad heart gay.
He sees thee, and calls to his gloomy train,
Thy sleet, and the snow, and the wind, and the rain;
And they shrink away, and they flee in fear,
When thy merry step draws near.

Winter giveth the fields and the trees, so old
Their beards of icicles and snow;
And the rain, it raineth so fast and cold,
We must cower over the embers low;
And, snugly housed from the wind and weather,
Mope like birds that are changing feather.
But the storm retires, and the sky grows clear,
When thy merry step draws near.

Winter maketh the sun in the gloomy sky
Wrap him round with a mantle of cloud;
But, Heaven be praised, thy step is nigh;
Thou tearest away the mournful shroud,
And the earth looks bright and Winter surly,
Who has toiled for nought both late and early.
Is banished afar by the new-born year,
When they merry step draws near.

Lines Written In Early Spring

William Wordsworth

I heard a thousand blended notes,
While in a grove I sate reclined,

In that sweet mood when pleasant thoughts
Bring sad thoughts to the mind.
To her fair works did Nature link
The human soul that through me ran;
And much it grieved my heart to think
What man has made of man.
Through primrose tufts, in that green bower,
The periwinkle trailed its wreaths;
And 'tis my faith that every flower
Enjoys the air it breathes.
The birds around me hopped and played,
Their thoughts I cannot measure:-
But the least motion which they made
It seemed a thrill of pleasure.
The budding twigs spread out their fan,
To catch the breezy air;
And I must think, do all I can,
That there was pleasure there.
If this belief from heaven be sent,
If such be Nature's holy plan,
Have I not reason to lament
What man has made of man?

#812
Emily Dickinson

A Light exists in Spring
Not present on the Year
At any other period —
When March is scarcely here

A Color stands abroad
On Solitary Fields

That Science cannot overtake
But Human Nature feels.

It waits upon the Lawn,
It shows the furthest Tree
Upon the furthest Slope you know
It almost speaks to you.

Then as Horizons step
Or Noons report away
Without the Formula of sound
It passes and we stay —

A quality of loss
Affecting our Content
As Trade had suddenly encroached
Upon a Sacrament.

Loveliest of Trees, the Cherry Now
A.E. Housman

Loveliest of trees, the cherry now
Is hung with bloom along the bough,
And stands about the woodland ride
Wearing white for Eastertide.

Now, of my threescore years and ten,
Twenty will not come again,
And take from seventy springs a score,
It only leaves me fifty more.

And since to look at things in bloom
Fifty springs are little room,

About the woodlands I will go
To see the cherry hung with snow.

The Furrow
Padraic Colum

Stride the hill, sower,
Up to the sky-ridge,
Flinging the seed,
Scattering, exultant!
Mouthing great rhythms
To the long sea beats
On the wide shore, behind
The ridge of the hillside.

Below in the darkness--
The slumber of mothers--
The cradles at rest--
The fire-seed sleeping
Deep in white ashes!

Give to darkness and sleep:
O sower, O seer!
Give me to the Earth.
With the seed I would enter.
O! the growth thro' the silence
From strength to new strength;
Then the strong bursting forth
Against primal forces,
To laugh in the sunshine,
To gladden the world!

Putting In the Seed
Robert Frost

You come to fetch me from my work to-night
When supper's on the table, and we'll see
If I can leave off burying the white
Soft petals fallen from the apple tree.
(Soft petals, yes, but not so barren quite,
Mingled with these, smooth bean and wrinkled pea;)
And go along with you ere you lose sight
Of what you came for and become like me,

Slave to a springtime passion for the earth.
How Love burns through the Putting in the Seed
On through the watching for that early birth
When, just as the soil tarnishes with weed,

The sturdy seedling with arched body comes
Shouldering its way and shedding the earth crumbs.

These, I, Singing In Spring
Walt Whitman

THESE, I, singing in spring, collect for lovers,
(For who but I should understand lovers, and all their sorrow and
joy?
And who but I should be the poet of comrades?)
Collecting, I traverse the garden, the world--but soon I pass the
gates,
Now along the pond-side--now wading in a little, fearing not the
wet,
Now by the post-and-rail fences, where the old stones thrown
there,

pick'd from the fields, have accumulated,
(Wild-flowers and vines and weeds come up through the stones, and
partly cover them--Beyond these I pass,)
Far, far in the forest, before I think where I go,
Solitary, smelling the earthy smell, stopping now and then in the silence,
Alone I had thought--yet soon a troop gathers around me,
Some walk by my side, and some behind, and some embrace my arms or
neck,
They, the spirits of dear friends, dead or alive--thicker they come, a great crowd, and I in the middle,
Collecting, dispensing, singing in spring, there I wander with them,
Plucking something for tokens--tossing toward whoever is near me;
Here! lilac, with a branch of pine,
Here, out of my pocket, some moss which I pull'd off a live-oak in Florida, as it hung trailing down,
Here, some pinks and laurel leaves, and a handful of sage,
And here what I now draw from the water, wading in the pond-side,
(O here I last saw him that tenderly loves me--and returns again, never to separate from me,
And this, O this shall henceforth be the token of comrades--this Calamus-root shall,
Interchange it, youths, with each other! Let none render it back!)
And twigs of maple, and a bunch of wild orange, and chestnut,
And stems of currants, and plum-blows, and the aromatic cedar:
These, I, compass'd around by a thick cloud of spirits,
Wandering, point to, or touch as I pass, or throw them loosely from
me,
Indicating to each one what he shall have--giving something to

---

each;
But what I drew from the water by the pond-side, that I reserve,
I will give of it--but only to them that love, as I myself am capable
of loving.

In A Garden
Horace Holley

I stood within a Garden during rain
Uncovering to the drops my lifted brow:
O joyous fancy, to imagine now
I slip, with trees and clouds, the social chain,
Alone with nature, naught to lose or gain
Nor even to become; no, just to be
A moment's personal essence, wholly free
From needs that mold the heart to forms of pain.
Arise, I cried, and celebrate the hour!
Acclaim serener gladness; if it fail,
New courage, nobler vision, will survive
That I have known my kinship to the flower,
My brotherhood with rain, and in this vale
Have been a moment's friend to all alive.

A Shower
Rowland Thirlmere

You may have seen, when winds were high,
That hesitant buds would not unfold
In garden-borders chill and dry,
Bright with the Easter-lilies' gold.

Then, suddenly, would come a shower--
The big breeze veering to the west--
And happier music filled the bower
Above the thrush's hidden nest:

The elm-tree's inconspicuous bloom
Vanished amidst her little leaves;
In box and bay a fragrant gloom
Inspired the wren's recitatives:

The woods assumed their delicate green
And spoke in songs that brought you bliss:
Ay, and your withered heart has been
Quickened on such a day as this!

Charm: To Be Said In the Sun

Josephine Preston Peabody

I reach my arms up, to the sky,
And golden vine on vine
Of sunlight showered wild and high,
Around my brows I twine.

I wreathe, I wind it everywhere,
The burning radiancy
Of brightness that no eye may dare,
To be the strength of me.

Come, redness of the crystalline,
Come green, come hither blue
And violet--all alive within,
For I have need of you.

Come honey-hue and flush of gold,
And through the pallor run,
With pulse on pulse of manifold
New largess of the Sun!

O steep the silence till it sing!
O glories from the height,
Come down, where I am garlanding
With light, a child of light!

Spring

John Gould Fletcher

At the first hour, it was as if one said, "Arise."
At the second hour, it was as if one said, "Go forth."
And the winter constellations that are like patient ox-eyes
Sank below the white horizon at the north.

At the third hour, it was as if one said, "I thirst;"
At the fourth hour, all the earth was still:
Then the clouds suddenly swung over, stooped, and burst;
And the rain flooded valley, plain and hill.

At the fifth hour, darkness took the throne;
At the sixth hour, the earth shook and the wind cried;
At the seventh hour, the hidden seed was sown,
At the eighth hour, it gave up the ghost and died.

At the ninth hour, they sealed up the tomb;
And the earth was then silent for the space of three hours.
But at the twelfth hour, a single lily from the gloom
Shot forth, and was followed by a whole host of flowers.

An April Morning
Bliss Carman

Once more in misted April
The world is growing green.
Along the winding river
The plumey willows lean.

Beyond the sweeping meadows
The looming mountains rise,
Like battlements of dreamland
Against the brooding skies.

In every wooded valley
The buds are breaking through,
As though the heart of all things
No languor ever knew.

The golden-wings and bluebirds
Call to their heavenly choirs.
The pines are blued and drifted
With smoke of brushwood fires.

And in my sister's garden
Where little breezes run,
The golden daffodillies
Are blowing in the sun.

April Rain
Conrad Aiken

Fall, rain! You are the blood of coming blossom,
You shall be music in the young birds' throats,

You shall be breaking, soon, in silver notes;
A virgin laughter in the young earth's bosom.
Oh, that I could with you reënter earth,
Pass through her heart and come again to sun,
Out of her fertile dark to sing and run
In loveliness and fragrance of new mirth!
Fall, rain! Into the dust I go with you,
Pierce the remaining snows with subtle fire,
Warming the frozen roots with soft desire,
Dreams of ascending leaves and flowers new.
I am no longer body,--I am blood
Seeking for some new loveliness of shape;
Dark loveliness that dreams of new escape,
The sun-surrender of unclosing bud.
Take me, O Earth! and make me what you will;
I feel my heart with mingled music fill.

Daffodils
Ruth Guthrie Harding

There flames the first gay daffodil
Where winter-long the snows have lain:
Who buried Love, all spent and still?
There flames the first gay daffodil.
Go, Love's alive on yonder hill,
And yours for asking, joy and pain,
There flames the first gay daffodil
Where winter-long the snows have lain!

A White Iris
Pauline B. Barrington

Tall and clothed in samite,
Chaste and pure,
In smooth armor,--
Your head held high
In its helmet
Of silver:
Jean D'Arc riding
Among the sword blades!

Has Spring for you
Wrought visions,
As it did for her
In a garden?

Beyond
Thomas S. Jones, Jr.

I wonder if the tides of Spring
  Will always bring me back again
Mute rapture at the simple thing
  Of lilacs blowing in the rain.

If so, my heart will ever be
  Above all fear, for I shall know
There is a greater mystery
  Beyond the time when lilacs blow.

Poems of Summer

Poems of Summer

Summer

from *The Second Pastoral* by Alexander Pope (1709)

See what Delights in Sylvan Scenes appear!
Descending Gods have found Elysium here.
In Woods bright Venus with Adonis stray'd;
And chast Diana haunts the Forest Shade.
Come lovely Nymph, and bless the silent Hours,
When Swains from Sheering seek their nightly Bow'rs;
When weary Reapers quit the sultry Field,
And crown'd with Corn, their Thanks to Ceres yield.
This harmless Grove no lurking Viper hides,
But in my Breast the Serpent Love abides.
Here Bees from Blossoms sip the rosy Dew,
But your Alexis knows no Sweet but you.
Some God conduct you to these blissful Seats,
The mossie Fountains, and the Green Retreats!
Where-e'er you walk, cool Gales shall fan the Glade,
Trees, where you sit, shall crowd into a Shade,
Where-e'er you tread, the blushing Flow'rs shall rise,
And all things flourish where you turn your Eyes.
Oh! how I long with you to pass my Days,
Invoke the Muses, and resound your Praise;
Your Praise the Birds shall chant in ev'ry Grove,
And Winds shall waft it to the Pow'rs above.
But would you sing, and rival Orpheus' Strain,
The wond'ring Forests soon shou'd dance again,
The moving Mountains hear the pow'rful Call,
And headlong Streams hang list'ning in their Fall!

But see, the Shepherds shun the Noon-day Heat,
The lowing Herds to murm'ring Brooks retreat,
To closer Shades the panting Flocks remove,
Ye Gods! and is there no Relief for Love?
But soon the Sun with milder Rays descends

To the cool Ocean, where his Journey ends;
On me Love's fiercer Flames for ever prey,
By Night he scorches, as he burns by Day.

A Summer Invocation

Walt Whitman (first published in *The American*, 1881)

Thou orb aloft full dazzling,
Flooding with sheeny light the gray beach sand;
Thou sibilant near sea, with vistas far, and foam,
And tawny streaks and shades, and spreading blue;
Before I sing the rest, O sun refulgent,
My special word to thee.

Hear me, illustrious!
Thy lover me—for always I have loved thee,
Even as basking babe—then happy boy alone by some wood
edge—thy touching distant beams enough,
Or man matured, or young or old—as now to thee I launch my in-
vocation.
(Thou canst not with thy dumbness me deceive.
I know before the fitting man all Nature yields.
Though answering not in words, the skies, trees, hear his voice—
and thou, O sun,
As for thy throes, thy perturbations, sudden breaks and shafts of
flame gigantic,
I understand them—I know those flames, those perturbations
well.)

Thou that with fructifying heat and light,
O'er myriad forms—o'er lands and waters, North and South,
O'er Mississippi's endless course, o'er Texas' grassy plains, Ka-
nada's woods,

O'er all the globe, that turns its face to thee, shining in space,
Thou that impartially enfoldest all—not only continents, seas,
Thou that to grapes and weeds and little wild flowers givest so liberally,
Shed, shed thyself on mine and me—mellow these lines.
Fuse thyself here—with but a fleeting ray out of thy million millions,
Strike through this chant.

Nor only launch thy subtle dazzle and thy strength for this;
Prepare the later afternoon of me myself—prepare my lengthening shadows.
Prepare my starry nights.

#122
Emily Dickinson

A something in a summer's Day
As slow her flambeaux burn away
Which solemnizes me.

A something in a summer's noon —
A depth — an Azure — a perfume —
Transcending ecstasy.

And still within a summer's night
A something so transporting bright
I clap my hands to see —

Then veil my too inspecting face
Lets such a subtle — shimmering grace
Flutter too far for me —

The wizard fingers never rest —

The purple brook within the breast
Still chafes it narrow bed —

Still rears the East her amber Flag —
Guides still the sun along the Crag
His Caravan of Red —

So looking on — the night — the morn
Conclude the wonder gay —
And I meet, coming thro' the dews
Another summer's Day!

Summer in the South
Paul Laurence Dunbar

The oriole sings in the greening grove
As if he were half-way waiting,
The rosebuds peep from their hoods of green,
Timid, and hesitating.
The rain comes down in a torrent sweep
And the nights smell warm and pinety,
The garden thrives, but the tender shoots
Are yellow-green and tiny.
Then a flash of sun on a waiting hill,
Streams laugh that erst were quiet,
The sky smiles down with a dazzling blue
And the woods run mad with riot.

To Summer
William Blake (from *Poetical Sketches*, 1783)

O thou who passest thro' our valleys in
Thy strength, curb thy fierce steeds, allay the heat
That flames from their large nostrils! thou, O Summer,

Oft pitchedst here thy golden tent, and oft
Beneath our oaks hast slept, while we beheld
With joy, thy ruddy limbs and flourishing hair.

Beneath our thickest shades we oft have heard
Thy voice, when noon upon his fervid car
Rode o'er the deep of heaven: beside our springs
Sit down, and in our mossy valleys, on
Some bank beside a river clear, throw thy
Silk draperies off, and rush into the stream:
Our valleys love the Summer in his pride.

Our bards are famed who strike the silver wire:
Our youth are bolder than the southern swains:
Our maidens fairer in the sprightly dance:
We lack not songs, nor instruments of joy,
Nor echoes sweet, nor waters clear as heaven,
Nor laurel wreaths against the sultry heat.

Summer Images

John Clare *(from The Rural Muse, 1835)*

Now swarthy Summer, by rude health embrowned,
Precedence takes of rosy fingered Spring;
And laughing Joy, with wild flowers prank'd, and crown'd,
A wild and giddy thing,
And Health robust, from every care unbound,
Come on the zephyr's wing,
And cheer the toiling clown.

Happy as holiday-enjoying face,
Loud tongued, and "merry as a marriage bell,"
Thy lightsome step sheds joy in every place;

And where the troubled dwell,
Thy witching charms wean them of half their cares;
And from thy sunny spell,
They greet joy unawares.

Then with thy sultry locks all loose and rude,
And mantle laced with gems of garish light,
Come as of wont; for I would fain intrude,
And in the world's despite,
Share the rude wealth that thy own heart beguiles;
If haply so I might
Win pleasure from thy smiles.

Me not the noise of brawling pleasure cheers,
In nightly revels or in city streets;
But joys which soothe, and not distract the ears,
That one at leisure meets
In the green woods, and meadows summer-shorn,
Or fields, where bee-fly greets
The ear with mellow horn.

The green-swathed grasshopper, on treble pipe,
Sings there, and dances, in mad-hearted pranks;
There bees go courting every flower that's ripe,
On baulks and sunny banks;
And droning dragon-fly, on rude bassoon,
Attempts to give God thanks
In no discordant tune.

The speckled thrush, by self-delight embued,
There sings unto himself for joy's amends,
And drinks the honey dew of solitude.
There Happiness attends
With inbred Joy until the heart o'erflow,
Of which the world's rude friends,

Nought heeding, nothing know.

There the gay river, laughing as it goes,
Plashes with easy wave its flaggy sides,
And to the calm of heart, in calmness shows
What pleasure there abides,
To trace its sedgy banks, from trouble free:
Spots Solitude provides
To muse, and happy be.

There ruminating 'neath some pleasant bush,
On sweet silk grass I stretch me at mine ease,
Where I can pillow on the yielding rush;
And, acting as I please,
Drop into pleasant dreams; or musing lie,
Mark the wind-shaken trees,
And cloud-betravelled sky.

There think me how some barter joy for care,
And waste life's summer-health in riot rude,
Of nature, nor of nature's sweets aware.
When passions vain intrude,
These, by calm musings, softened are and still;
And the heart's better mood
Feels sick of doing ill.

There I can live, and at my leisure seek
Joys far from cold restraints—not fearing pride—
Free as the winds, that breathe upon my cheek
Rude health, so long denied.
Here poor Integrity can sit at ease,
And list self-satisfied
The song of honey-bees.

The green lane now I traverse, where it goes

Nought guessing, till some sudden turn espies
Rude batter'd finger post, that stooping shows
Where the snug mystery lies;
And then a mossy spire, with ivy crown,
Cheers up the short surprise,
And shows a peeping town.

I see the wild flowers, in their summer morn
Of beauty, feeding on joy's luscious hours;
The gay convolvulus, wreathing round the thorn,
Agape for honey showers;
And slender kingcup, burnished with the dew
Of morning's early hours,
Like gold yminted new.

And mark by rustic bridge, o'er shallow stream,
Cow-tending boy, to toil unreconciled,
Absorbed as in some vagrant summer dream;
Who now, in gestures wild,
Starts dancing to his shadow on the wall,
Feeling self-gratified,
Nor fearing human thrall.

Or thread the sunny valley laced with streams,
Or forests rude, and the o'ershadow'd brims
Of simple ponds, where idle shepherd dreams,
Stretching his listless limbs;
Or trace hay-scented meadows, smooth and long,
Where joy's wild impulse swims
In one continued song.

I love at early morn, from new mown swath,
To see the startled frog his route pursue;
To mark while, leaping o'er the dripping path,
His bright sides scatter dew,

The early lark that from its bustle flies,
To hail his matin new;
And watch him to the skies.

To note on hedgerow baulks, in moisture sprent,
The jetty snail creep from the mossy thorn,
With earnest heed, and tremulous intent,
Frail brother of the morn,
That from the tiny bent's dew-misted leaves
Withdraws his timid horn,
And fearful vision weaves.

Or swallow heed on smoke-tanned chimney top,
Wont to be first unsealing Morning's eye,
Ere yet the bee hath gleaned one wayward drop
Of honey on his thigh;
To see him seek morn's airy couch to sing,
Until the golden sky
Bepaint his russet wing.

Or sauntering boy by tanning corn to spy,
With clapping noise to startle birds away,
And hear him bawl to every passer by
To know the hour of day;
While the uncradled breezes, fresh and strong,
With waking blossoms play,
And breathe Æolian song.

I love the south-west wind, or low or loud,
And not the less when sudden drops of rain
Moisten my glowing cheek from ebon cloud,
Threatening soft showers again,
That over lands new ploughed and meadow grounds,
Summer's sweet breath unchain,
And wake harmonious sounds.

Rich music breathes in Summer's every sound;
And in her harmony of varied greens,
Woods, meadows, hedge-rows, corn-fields, all around
Much beauty intervenes,
Filling with harmony the ear and eye;
While o'er the mingling scenes
Far spreads the laughing sky.

See, how the wind-enamoured aspen leaves
Turn up their silver lining to the sun!
And hark! the rustling noise, that oft deceives,
And makes the sheep-boy run:
The sound so mimics fast-approaching showers,
He thinks the rain's begun,
And hastes to sheltering bowers.

But now the evening curdles dank and grey,
Changing her watchet hue for sombre weed;
And moping owls, to close the lids of day,
On drowsy wing proceed;
While chickering crickets, tremulous and long,
Light's farewell inly heed,
And give it parting song.

The pranking bat its flighty circlet makes;
The glow-worm burnishes its lamp anew;
O'er meadows dew-besprent, the beetle wakes
Inquiries ever new,
Teazing each passing ear with murmurs vain,
As wanting to pursue
His homeward path again.

Hark! 'tis the melody of distant bells
That on the wind with pleasing hum rebounds
By fitful starts, then musically swells
O'er the dim stilly grounds;

While on the meadow-bridge the pausing boy
Listens the mellow sounds,
And hums in vacant joy.

How sweet the soothing calmness that distills
O'er the heart's every sense its opiate dews,
In meek-eyed moods and ever balmy trills!
That softens and subdues,
With gentle Quiet's bland and sober train,
Which dreamy eve renews
In many a mellow strain!

I love to walk the fields, they are to me
A legacy no evil can destroy;
They, like a spell, set every rapture free
That cheer'd me when a boy.
Play—pastime—all Time's blotting pen conceal'd,
Comes like a new-born joy,
To greet me in the field.

For Nature's objects ever harmonize
With emulous Taste, that vulgar deed annoys;
Which loves in pensive moods to sympathize,
And meet vibrating joys
O'er Nature's pleasing things; nor slighting, deems
Pastimes, the Muse employs,
Vain and obtrusive themes.

The Summer Rain

Henry David Thoreau

My books I'd fain cast off, I cannot read,
'Twixt every page my thoughts go stray at large
Down in the meadow, where is richer feed,
And will not mind to hit their proper targe.

Plutarch was good, and so was Homer too,
Our Shakespeare's life were rich to live again,
What Plutarch read, that was not good nor true,
Nor Shakespeare's books, unless his books were men.

Here while I lie beneath this walnut bough,
What care I for the Greeks or for Troy town,
If juster battles are enacted now
Between the ants upon this hummock's crown?

Bid Homer wait till I the issue learn,
If red or black the gods will favor most,
Or yonder Ajax will the phalanx turn,
Struggling to heave some rock against the host.

Tell Shakespeare to attend some leisure hour,
For now I've business with this drop of dew,
And see you not, the clouds prepare a shower—
I'll meet him shortly when the sky is blue.

This bed of herd's grass and wild oats was spread
Last year with nicer skill than monarchs use.
A clover tuft is pillow for my head,
And violets quite overtop my shoes.

And now the cordial clouds have shut all in,
And gently swells the wind to say all's well;

The scattered drops are falling fast and thin,
Some in the pool, some in the flower-bell.

I am well drenched upon my bed of oats;
But see that globe come rolling down its stem,
Now like a lonely planet there it floats,
And now it sinks into my garment's hem.

Drip drip the trees for all the country round,
And richness rare distills from every bough;
The wind alone it is makes every sound,
Shaking down crystals on the leaves below.

For shame the sun will never show himself,
Who could not with his beams e'er melt me so;
My dripping locks—they would become an elf,
Who in a beaded coat does gayly go.

Warble for Lilac-Time

Walt Whitman (from *Leaves of Grass*, first published in 1871 edition)

Warble me now for joy of lilac-time, (returning in reminiscence,)
Sort me O tongue and lips for Nature's sake, souvenirs of earliest summer,
Gather the welcome signs, (as children with pebbles or stringing shells,)
Put in April and May, the hylas croaking in the ponds, the elastic air,
Bees, butterflies, the sparrow with its simple notes,
Blue-bird and darting swallow, nor forget the high-hole flashing his golden wings,
The tranquil sunny haze, the clinging smoke, the vapor,

Shimmer of waters with fish in them, the cerulean above,
All that is jocund and sparkling, the brooks running,
The maple woods, the crisp February days and the sugar-making,
The robin where he hops, bright-eyed, brown-breasted,
With musical clear call at sunrise, and again at sunset,
Or flitting among the trees of the apple-orchard, building the nest
of his mate,
The melted snow of March, the willow sending forth its yellow-
green sprouts,
For spring-time is here! the summer is here! and what is this in it
and from it?
Thou, soul, unloosen'd—the restlessness after I know not what;
Come, let us lag here no longer, let us be up and away!
O if one could but fly like a bird!
O to escape, to sail forth as in a ship!
To glide with thee O soul, o'er all, in all, as a ship o'er the waters;
Gathering these hints, the preludes, the blue sky, the grass, the
morning drops of dew,
The lilac-scent, the bushes with dark green heart-shaped leaves,
Wood-violets, the little delicate pale blossoms called innocence,
Samples and sorts not for themselves alone, but for their atmos-
phere,
To grace the bush I love—to sing with the birds,
A warble for joy of lilac-time, returning in reminiscence.

#794
Emily Dickinson

A Drop Fell on the Apple Tree —
Another — on the Roof —
A Half a Dozen kissed the Eaves —
And made the Gables laugh —

A few went out to help the Brook
That went to help the Sea —
Myself Conjectured were they Pearls —
What Necklace could be —

The Dust replaced, in Hoisted Roads —
The Birds jocoser sung —
The Sunshine threw his Hat away —
The Bushes — spangles flung —

The Breezes brought dejected Lutes —
And bathed them in the Glee —
Then Orient showed a single Flag,
And signed the Fete away —

In Summer

Paul Laurence Dunbar (from *Lyrics of the Hearthside*, 1899)

Oh, summer has clothed the earth
In a cloak from the loom of the sun!
And a mantle, too, of the skies' soft blue,
And a belt where the rivers run.

And now for the kiss of the wind,
And the touch of the air's soft hands,
With the rest from strife and the heat of life,
With the freedom of lakes and lands.

I envy the farmer's boy
Who sings as he follows the plow;
While the shining green of the young blades lean
To the breezes that cool his brow.

He sings to the dewy morn,
No thought of another's ear;
But the song he sings is a chant for kings
And the whole wide world to hear.

He sings of the joys of life,
Of the pleasures of work and rest,
From an o'erfull heart, without aim or art;
'T is a song of the merriest.

O ye who toil in the town,
And ye who moil in the mart,
Hear the artless song, and your faith made strong
Shall renew your joy of heart.

Oh, poor were the worth of the world
If never a song were heard, —
If the sting of grief had no relief,
And never a heart were stirred.

So, long as the streams run down,
And as long as the robins trill,
Let us taunt old Care with a merry air,
And sing in the face of ill.

Prelude to Part First, The Vision of Sir Launfal

James Russell Lowell

Over his keys the musing organist,
Beginning doubtfully and far away,
First lets his fingers wander as they list,
And builds a bridge from Dreamland for his lay:
Then, as the touch of his loved instrument
Gives hope and fervor, nearer draws his theme,
First guessed by faint auroral flushes sent

Along the wavering vista of his dream.

Not only around our infancy
Doth heaven with all its splendors lie;
Daily, with souls that cringe and plot,
We Sinais, climb and know it not.

Over our manhood bend the skies;
Against our fallen and traitor lives
The great winds utter prophecies;
With our faint hearts the mountain strives;
Its arms outstretched, the druid wood
Waits with its benedicite;
And to our age's drowsy blood
Still shouts the inspiring sea.

Earth gets its price for what Earth gives us;
The beggar is taxed for a corner to die in,
The priest hath his fee who comes and shrives us,
We bargain for the graves we lie in:
At the Devil's booth are all things sold,
Each ounce of dross costs its ounce of gold;
For a cap and bells our lives we pay,
Bubbles we buy with a whole soul's tasking
'T is heaven alone that is given away,
'T is only God may be had for the asking;
No price is set on the lavish summer;
June may be had by the poorest comer.

And what is so rare as a day in June?
Then, if ever, come perfect days;
Then Heaven tries the earth if it be in tune,
And over it softly her warm ear lays:
Whether we look, or whether we listen,
We hear life murmur, or see it glisten;

Every clod feels a stir of might,
An instinct within it that reaches and towers,
And, groping blindly above it for light,
Climbs to a soul in grass and flowers;
The flush of life may well be seen
Thrilling back over hills and valleys;
The cowslip startles in meadows green,
The buttercup catches the sun in its chalice,
And there's never a leaf nor a blade too mean
To be some happy creature's palace;
The little bird sits at his door in the sun,
Atilt like a blossom among the leaves,
And lets his illumined being o'errun
With the deluge of summer it receives;
His mate feels the eggs beneath her wings,
And the heart in her dumb breast flutters and sings;
He sings to the wide world, and she to her nest,—
In the nice ear of Nature which song is the best?

Now is the high-tide of the year
And whatever of life hath ebbed away
Comes flooding back, with a ripply cheer,
Into every bare inlet and creek and bay;
Now the heart is so full that a drop overfills it,
We are happy now, because God wills it;
No matter how barren the past may have been,
'T is enough for us now that the leaves are green;
We sit in the warm shade and feel right well
How the sap creeps up and the blossoms swell;
We may shut our eyes, but we cannot help knowing
That skies are clear and grass is growing:
The breeze comes whispering in our ear
That dandelions are blossoming near,
That maize has sprouted, that streams are flowing,
That the river is bluer than the sky,

That the robin is plastering his house hard by;
And if the breeze kept the good news back,
For other couriers we should not lack;
We could guess it all by yon heifer's lowing, —
And hark! how clear bold chanticleer,
Warmed with the new wine of the year,
Tells all in his lusty crowing!

Joy comes, grief goes, we know not how;
Everything is happy now,
Everything is upward striving;
'T is as easy now for the heart to be true
As for grass to be green or skies to be blue, —
'T is the natural way of living:
Who knows whither the clouds have fled?
I n the unscarred heaven they leave no wake;
And the eyes forget the tears they have shed,
The heart forgets its sorrow and ache;
The soul partakes the season's youth,
And the sulphurous rifts of passion and woe
Lie deep 'neath a silence pure and smooth,
Like burnt-out craters healed with snow.
What wonder if Sir Launfal now
Remembered the keeping of his vow?

Summer
Edward Carpenter

Dreaming all day, as of old, in the far-off heights of
the sky.

The summer floats orbed in gold, while the hours
speed silently by;

The clouds are clad as in dreams, and the air is girt
with a sleep,

And the sound of its swaying seems like the wistful
sigh of the deep.

The forests stand dark in the sun, and the meadows
are bright between.

All gathered and melted in one, like a veil of
luminous sheen.

And rolled, as a wonderful weft, o'er the purple
shoulder of Earth,

Or a bridal vesture left from moments of music
and mirth.

So all is still in the vale, all silent aloft on the wold;
The trees have forgotten their tale, the mystical
murmur of old;

All sound of music is done in sky and meadow and glade,
And the whole wood sleeps in the sun, where the
sunlight sleeps in the shade.

The drowsy tips of the leaves are dipped in the heat,
as a flood,

And their idle dalliance weaves strange magic of
sleep in the blood;

Through the tall grass spreadeth the spell and the
hours are charmed to rest —

O the spirit of Spring is well, but the silence of
Summer is best

Poppies
John Russell Hayes

O perfect flowers of sweet midsummer days,
  The season's emblems ye,
  As nodding lazily
Ye kiss to sleep each breeze that near you strays,
  And soothe the tired gazer's sense
    With lulling surges of your softest somnolence
Like fairy lamps ye light the garden bed
  With tender ruby glow.
  Not any flowers that blow
Can match the glory of your gleaming red;
  Such sunny-warm and dreamy hue
Before ye lit your fires no garden ever knew.
Bright are the blossoms of the scarlet sage,
  And bright the velvet vest
  On the nasturtium's breast;
Bright are the tulips when they reddest rage,
  And bright the coreopsis' eye;--
But none of all can with your brilliant beauty vie.
O soft and slumberous flowers, we love you well;
  Your glorious crimson tide
  The mossy walk beside
Holds all the garden in its drowsy spell;
  And walking there we gladly bless
Your queenly grace and all your languorous loveliness.

The Garden In August

Gertrude Huntington McGiffert

From corn-crib by the level pasture-lands
To knoll where spruce and boulders hide the road
I know it like a book, and when my heart
Is waste and dry and hard and choked with weeds,
I come here till it gently blooms again.
For gardens yield rich fruits that will outlast
The autumn and the winter of the soul,
Richest to him who toils with loving hands.
'Tis delving thus we learn life's secrets told
But to those favored few who dig for them.
The Garden is an intimate and keeps
In touch with us, yet hath its own high moods,
And doth impose them on the mind of man
To shame his pettiness. So do I love
Its shimmering August mood keyed to the sun,
A harlequin of color, birds and bloom.
Nasturtiums, zinnias, balsams, salvias blaze
By vivid dahlias; tiger-lilies burn
In scarlet shadow of Jerusalem-cross;
Beyond the queen-hydrangeas splendid rule
Barbaric marigolds; chrysanthemums
Outshine gladioli, and sunflowers flaunt
Their crests of gold beneath the giant gourds.
Within the arbor, script forgot, I muse,
While gorgeous hollyhocks sway to and fro
To mark the silences, and butterflies
Flit in and out like some bright memory,
And blinding poppies kindle slow watch-fires
Before the golden altar of the sun.
A spell lies on the Garden. Summer sits
With finger on her lips as if she heard
The steps of Autumn echo on the hill.

A hush lies on the Garden. Summer dreams
Of timid crocus thrust through drifted snow.

Sun, Cardinal, and Corn Flowers
Hannah Parker Kimball

Whence gets Earth her gold for thee,
O Sunflower?
Her woven, yellow locks so fine
Must go to make that gold of thine.

And whence thy red beside the stream,
O Cardinal-flower?
She pricks some vein lies near her heart
That thy rich, ruddy hue may start.

And whence thy blue amid the corn,
O Corn-flower?
Her deep-blue eyes gleam out in glee,
The glories of her work to see.

Sunflowers
Clinton Scollard

My tall sunflowers love the sun,
  Love the burning August noons
When the locust tunes its viol,
  And the cricket croons.

When the purple night draws on,
  With its planets hung on high,
And the attared winds of slumber
  Wander down the sky,

Still my sunflowers love the sun,
  Keep their ward and watch and wait
Till the rosy key of morning
  Opes the eastern gate.

Then, when they have deeply quaffed
  From the brimming cups of dew,
You can hear their golden laughter
  All the garden through.

The End of Summer
Edna St. Vincent Millay

When poppies in the garden bleed,
And coreopsis goes to seed,
And pansies, blossoming past their prime,
Grow small and smaller all the time,
When on the mown field, shrunk and dry,
Brown dock and purple thistle lie,
And smoke from forest fires at noon
Can make the sun appear the moon,
When apple seeds, all white before,
Begin to darken in the core,
I know that summer, scarcely here,
Is gone until another year.

Poems of Fall

A Late Walk
Robert Frost

When I go up through the mowing field,
 The headless aftermath,
Smooth-laid like thatch with the heavy dew,
 Half closes the garden path.

And when I come to the garden ground,
 The whir of sober birds
Up from the tangle of the withered weeds
 Is sadder than any words.

A tree beside the wall stands bare,
 But a leaf that lingered brown,
Disturbed, I doubt not, by my thought,
 Comes softly rustling down.

I end not far from my going forth
 By picking the faded blue
Of the last remaining aster flower
 To carry again to you.

Sonnet 73
William Shakespeare

That time of year thou mayst in me behold
When yellow leaves, or none, or few, do hang
Upon those boughs which shake against the cold,
Bare ruined choirs, where late the sweet birds sang.
In me thou see'st the twilight of such day
As after sunset fadeth in the west;
Which by and by black night doth take away,

Death's second self, that seals up all in rest.
In me thou see'st the glowing of such fire,
That on the ashes of his youth doth lie,
As the deathbed whereon it must expire,
Consumed with that which it was nourished by.
This thou perceiv'st, which makes thy love more strong,
To love that well which thou must leave ere long.

To Autumn
William Blake

O Autumn, laden with fruit, and stain'd
With the blood of the grape, pass not, but sit
Beneath my shady roof; there thou may'st rest,
And tune thy jolly voice to my fresh pipe,
And all the daughters of the year shall dance!
Sing now the lusty song of fruits and flowers.

"The narrow bud opens her beauties to
The sun, and love runs in her thrilling veins;
Blossoms hang round the brows of Morning, and
Flourish down the bright cheek of modest Eve,
Till clust'ring Summer breaks forth into singing,
And feather'd clouds strew flowers round her head.

"The spirits of the air live in the smells
Of fruit; and Joy, with pinions light, roves round
The gardens, or sits singing in the trees."
Thus sang the jolly Autumn as he sat,
Then rose, girded himself, and o'er the bleak
Hills fled from our sight; but left his golden load.

Spontaneous Me

Walt Whitman

Spontaneous me, Nature,
The loving day, the mounting sun, the friend I am happy with,
The arm of my friend hanging idly over my shoulder,
The hillside whiten'd with blossoms of the mountain ash,
The same late in autumn, the hues of red, yellow, drab, purple,
and
light and dark green,
The rich coverlet of the grass, animals and birds, the private
untrimm'd bank, the primitive apples, the pebble-stones,
Beautiful dripping fragments, the negligent list of one after
another as I happen to call them to me or think of them,
The real poems, (what we call poems being merely pictures,)
The poems of the privacy of the night, and of men like me,
This poem drooping shy and unseen that I always carry, and that
all
men carry,
(Know once for all, avow'd on purpose, wherever are men like me,
are
our lusty lurking masculine poems,)
Love-thoughts, love-juice, love-odor, love-yielding, love-climbers,
and the climbing sap,
Arms and hands of love, lips of love, phallic thumb of love, breasts
of love, bellies press'd and glued together with love,
Earth of chaste love, life that is only life after love,
The body of my love, the body of the woman I love, the body of
the
man, the body of the earth,
Soft forenoon airs that blow from the south-west,
The hairy wild-bee that murmurs and hankers up and down, that
gripes the
full-grown lady-flower, curves upon her with amorous firm legs,
takes

his will of her, and holds himself tremulous and tight till he is
satisfied;
The wet of woods through the early hours,
Two sleepers at night lying close together as they sleep, one with
an arm slanting down across and below the waist of the other,
The smell of apples, aromas from crush'd sage-plant, mint, birch-
bark,
The boy's longings, the glow and pressure as he confides to me
what
he was dreaming,
The dead leaf whirling its spiral whirl and falling still and
content to the ground,
The no-form'd stings that sights, people, objects, sting me with,
The hubb'd sting of myself, stinging me as much as it ever can any
one,
The sensitive, orbic, underlapp'd brothers, that only privileged
feelers may be intimate where they are,
The curious roamer the hand roaming all over the body, the bash-
ful
withdrawing of flesh where the fingers soothingly pause and
edge themselves,
The limpid liquid within the young man,
The vex'd corrosion so pensive and so painful,
The torment, the irritable tide that will not be at rest,
The like of the same I feel, the like of the same in others,
The young man that flushes and flushes, and the young woman
that
flushes and flushes,
The young man that wakes deep at night, the hot hand seeking to
repress what would master him,
The mystic amorous night, the strange half-welcome pangs, vi-
sions, sweats,
The pulse pounding through palms and trembling encircling fin-
gers,
the young man all color'd, red, ashamed, angry;

The souse upon me of my lover the sea, as I lie willing and naked,
The merriment of the twin babes that crawl over the grass in the
sun, the mother never turning her vigilant eyes from them,
The walnut-trunk, the walnut-husks, and the ripening or ripen'd
long-round walnuts,
The continence of vegetables, birds, animals,
The consequent meanness of me should I skulk or find myself in-
decent,
while birds and animals never once skulk or find themselves inde-
cent,
The great chastity of paternity, to match the great chastity of ma-
ternity,
The oath of procreation I have sworn, my Adamic and fresh
daughters,
The greed that eats me day and night with hungry gnaw, till I satu-
rate
what shall produce boys to fill my place when I am through,
The wholesome relief, repose, content,
And this bunch pluck'd at random from myself,
It has done its work--I toss it carelessly to fall where it may.

To Autumn
John Keats

Season of mists and mellow fruitfulness,
Close bosom-friend of the maturing sun;
Conspiring with him how to load and bless
With fruit the vines that round the thatch-eves run;
To bend with apples the moss'd cottage-trees,
And fill all fruit with ripeness to the core;
To swell the gourd, and plump the hazel shells
With a sweet kernel; to set budding more,
And still more, later flowers for the bees,

Until they think warm days will never cease,
For Summer has o'er-brimm'd their clammy cells.

Who hath not seen thee oft amid thy store?
Sometimes whoever seeks abroad may find
Thee sitting careless on a granary floor,
Thy hair soft-lifted by the winnowing wind;
Or on a half-reap'd furrow sound asleep,
Drows'd with the fume of poppies, while thy hook
Spares the next swath and all its twined flowers:
And sometimes like a gleaner thou dost keep
Steady thy laden head across a brook;
Or by a cyder-press, with patient look,
Thou watchest the last oozings hours by hours.

Where are the songs of Spring? Ay, where are they?
Think not of them, thou hast thy music too,—
While barred clouds bloom the soft-dying day,
And touch the stubble-plains with rosy hue;
Then in a wailful choir the small gnats mourn
Among the river sallows, borne aloft
Or sinking as the light wind lives or dies;
And full-grown lambs loud bleat from hilly bourn;
Hedge-crickets sing; and now with treble soft
The red-breast whistles from a garden-croft;
And gathering swallows twitter in the skies.

Ode to the West Wind
Percy Bysshe Shelley

I

O wild West Wind, thou breath of Autumn's being,

Thou, from whose unseen presence the leaves dead
Are driven, like ghosts from an enchanter fleeing,

Yellow, and black, and pale, and hectic red,
Pestilence-stricken multitudes: O thou,
Who chariotest to their dark wintry bed

The winged seeds, where they lie cold and low,
Each like a corpse within its grave, until
Thine azure sister of the Spring shall blow

Her clarion o'er the dreaming earth, and fill
(Driving sweet buds like flocks to feed in air)
With living hues and odours plain and hill:

Wild Spirit, which art moving everywhere;
Destroyer and preserver; hear, oh hear!

II

Thou on whose stream, mid the steep sky's commotion,
Loose clouds like earth's decaying leaves are shed,
Shook from the tangled boughs of Heaven and Ocean,

Angels of rain and lightning: there are spread
On the blue surface of thine aëry surge,
Like the bright hair uplifted from the head

Of some fierce Maenad, even from the dim verge
Of the horizon to the zenith's height,
The locks of the approaching storm. Thou dirge

Of the dying year, to which this closing night
Will be the dome of a vast sepulchre,

Vaulted with all thy congregated might

Of vapours, from whose solid atmosphere
Black rain, and fire, and hail will burst: oh hear!

III

Thou who didst waken from his summer dreams
The blue Mediterranean, where he lay,
Lull'd by the coil of his crystàlline streams,

Beside a pumice isle in Baiae's bay,
And saw in sleep old palaces and towers
Quivering within the wave's intenser day,

All overgrown with azure moss and flowers
So sweet, the sense faints picturing them! Thou
For whose path the Atlantic's level powers

Cleave themselves into chasms, while far below
The sea-blooms and the oozy woods which wear
The sapless foliage of the ocean, know

Thy voice, and suddenly grow gray with fear,
And tremble and despoil themselves: oh hear!

IV

If I were a dead leaf thou mightest bear;
If I were a swift cloud to fly with thee;
A wave to pant beneath thy power, and share

The impulse of thy strength, only less free

Than thou, O uncontrollable! If even
I were as in my boyhood, and could be

The comrade of thy wanderings over Heaven,
As then, when to outstrip thy skiey speed
Scarce seem'd a vision; I would ne'er have striven

As thus with thee in prayer in my sore need.
Oh, lift me as a wave, a leaf, a cloud!
I fall upon the thorns of life! I bleed!

A heavy weight of hours has chain'd and bow'd
One too like thee: tameless, and swift, and proud.

V

Make me thy lyre, even as the forest is:
What if my leaves are falling like its own!
The tumult of thy mighty harmonies

Will take from both a deep, autumnal tone,
Sweet though in sadness. Be thou, Spirit fierce,
My spirit! Be thou me, impetuous one!

Drive my dead thoughts over the universe
Like wither'd leaves to quicken a new birth!
And, by the incantation of this verse,

Scatter, as from an unextinguish'd hearth
Ashes and sparks, my words among mankind!
Be through my lips to unawaken'd earth

The trumpet of a prophecy! O Wind,
If Winter comes, can Spring be far behind?

Autumn

John Clare

The summer-flower has run to seed,
And yellow is the woodland bough;
And every leaf of bush and weed
Is tipt with autumn's pencil now.

And I do love the varied hue,
And I do love the browning plain;
And I do love each scene to view,
That's mark'd with beauties of her reign.

The woodbine-trees red berries bear,
That clustering hang upon the bower;
While, fondly lingering here and there,
Peeps out a dwindling sickly flower.

The trees' gay leaves are turned brown,
By every little wind undress'd;
And as they flap and whistle down,
We see the birds' deserted nest.

No thrush or blackbird meets the eye,
Or fills the ear with summer's strain;
They but dart out for worm and fly,
Then silent seek their rest again.

Beside the brook, in misty blue,
Bilberries glow on tendrils weak,
Where many a bare-foot splashes through,
The pulpy, juicy prize to seek:

For 'tis the rustic boy's delight,
Now autumn's sun so warmly gleams,

And these ripe berries tempt his sight,
To dabble in the shallow streams.

And oft his rambles we may trace,
Delv'd in the mud his printing feet,
And oft we meet a chubby face
All stained with the berries sweet.

The cowboy oft slives down the brook,
And tracks for hours each winding round,
While pinders, that such chances look,
Drive his rambling cows to pound.

The woodland bowers, that us'd to be
Lost in their silence and their shade,
Are now a scene of rural glee,
With many a nutting swain and maid.

The scrambling shepherd with his hook,
'Mong hazel boughs of rusty brown
That overhang some gulphing brook,
Drags the ripen'd clusters down.

While, on a bank of faded grass,
Some artless maid the prize receives;
And kisses to the sun-tann'd lass,
As well as nuts, the shepherd gives.

I love the year's decline, and love
Through rustling yellow shades to range,
O'er stubble land, 'neath willow grove,
To pause upon each varied change:

And oft have thought 'twas sweet, to list
The stubbles crackling with the heat,

Just as the sun broke through the mist
And warm'd the herdsman's rushy seat;

And grunting noise of rambling hogs,
Where pattering acorns oddly drop;
And noisy bark of shepherds' dogs,
The restless routs of sheep to stop;

While distant thresher's swingle drops
With sharp and hollow-twanking raps;
And, nigh at hand, the echoing chops
Of hardy hedger stopping gaps;

And sportsmen's trembling whistle-calls
That stay the swift retreating pack;
And cowboy's whoops, and squawking brawls,
To urge the straggling heifer back.

Autumn-time, thy scenes and shades
Are pleasing to the tasteful eye;
Though winter, when the thought pervades,
Creates an ague-shivering sigh.

Grey-bearded rime hangs on the morn,
And what's to come too true declares;
The ice-drop hardens on the thorn,
And winter's starving bed prepares.

No music's heard the fields among;
Save where the hedge-chats chittering play,
And ploughman drawls his lonely song,
As cutting short the dreary day.

Now shatter'd shades let me attend,
Reflecting look on their decline,

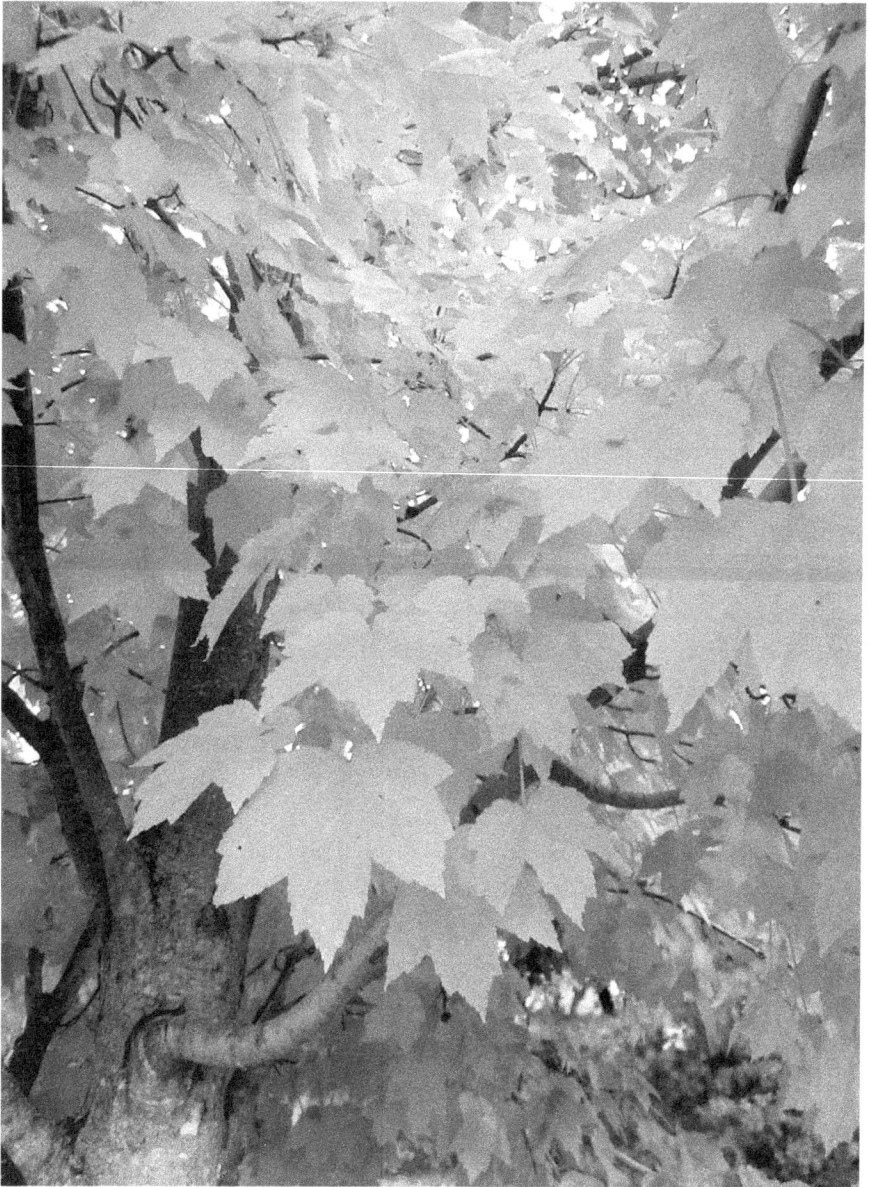

Where pattering leaves confess their end,
In sighing flutterings hinting mine.

For every leaf, that twirls the breeze,
May useful hints and lessons give;
The falling leaves and fading trees
Will teach and caution us to live.

"Wandering clown," they seem to say,
"In us your coming end review:
Like you we lived, but now decay;
The same sad fate approaches you."

Beneath a yellow fading tree,
As red suns light thee, Autumn-morn,
In wildest rapture let me see
The sweets that most thy charms adorn.

O while my eye the landscape views,
What countless beauties are display'd;
What varied tints of nameless hues, —
Shades endless melting into shade.

A russet red the hazels gain,
As suited to their drear decline;
While maples brightest dress retain,
And in the gayest yellows shine.

The poplar tree hath lost its pride;
Its leaves in wan consumption pine;
They hoary turn on either side,
And life to every gale resign.

The stubborn oak, with haughty pride
Still in its lingering green, we view;

But vain the strength he shows is tried,
He tinges slow with sickly hue.

The proudest triumph art conceives,
Or beauties nature's power can crown,
Grey-bearded time in shatters leaves;
Destruction's trample treads them down.

Tis lovely now to turn one's eye,
The changing face of heaven to mind;
How thin-spun clouds glide swiftly by,
While lurking storms slow move behind.

Now suns are clear, now clouds pervade,
Each moment chang'd, and chang'd again;
And first a light, and then a shade,
Swift glooms and brightens o'er the plain.

Poor pussy through the stubble flies,
In vain, o'erpowering foes to shun;
The lurking spaniel points the prize,
And pussy's harmless race is run.

The crowing pheasant, in the brakes,
Betrays his lair with awkward squalls;
A certain aim the gunner takes,
He clumsy fluskers up, and falls.

But hide thee, muse, the woods among,
Nor stain thy artless, rural rhymes;
Go leave the murderer's wiles unsung,
Nor mark the harden'd gunner's crimes.

The fields all clear'd, the labouring mice
To sheltering hedge and wood patrole,

Where hips and haws for food suffice,
That chumbled lie about their hole.

The squirrel, bobbing from the eye,
Is busy now about his hoard,
And in old nest of crow or pye
His winter-store is oft explor'd.

The leaves forsake the willow grey,
And down the brook they whirl and wind;
So hopes and pleasures whirl away,
And leave old age and pain behind.

The thorns and briars, vermilion-hue,
Now full of hips and haws are seen;
If village-prophecies be true,
They prove that winter will be keen.

Hark! started are some lonely strains:
The robin-bird is urg'd to sing;
Of chilly evening he complains,
And dithering droops his ruffled wing.

Slow o'er the wood the puddock sails;
And mournful, as the storms arise,
His feeble note of sorrow wails
To the unpitying frowning skies.

More coldly blows the autumn-breeze;
Old winter grins a blast between;
The north-winds rise and strip the trees,
And desolation shuts the scene.

The Autumn
Elizabeth Barrett Browning

Go, sit upon the lofty hill,
And turn your eyes around,
Where waving woods and waters wild
Do hymn an autumn sound.
The summer sun is faint on them —
The summer flowers depart —
Sit still — as all transform'd to stone,
Except your musing heart.

How there you sat in summer-time,
May yet be in your mind;
And how you heard the green woods sing
Beneath the freshening wind.
Though the same wind now blows around,
You would its blast recall;
For every breath that stirs the trees,
Doth cause a leaf to fall.

Oh! like that wind, is all the mirth
That flesh and dust impart:
We cannot bear its visitings,
When change is on the heart.
Gay words and jests may make us smile,
When Sorrow is asleep;
But other things must make us smile,
When Sorrow bids us weep!

The dearest hands that clasp our hands, —
Their presence may be o'er;
The dearest voice that meets our ear,
That tone may come no more!
Youth fades; and then, the joys of youth,

Which once refresh'd our mind,
Shall come — as, on those sighing woods,
The chilling autumn wind.

Hear not the wind — view not the woods;
Look out o'er vale and hill —
In spring, the sky encircled them —
The sky is round them still.
Come autumn's scathe — come winter's cold —
Come change — and human fate!
Whatever prospect Heaven doth bound,
Can ne'er be desolate.

Color Notes
Charles Wharton Stork

The brown of fallen leaves,
   The duller brown
   Of withered moss
Stubble and bared sheaves,
And pale light filtering down
The fields across.

The gray of slender trees,
The softer gray
Of melting skies.
What sobering ecstasies
One drinks on such a day
With chastened eyes!

The Golden Bowl
Mart McMillam

I stand upon the broad and rounded summit
Of a high hill
In the full golden flood of an October day
Nearing to twilight.
Below lie bouquets of woods, flat fields,
White strings of roads winding like fairy tales into the distance,
All steeped in sapphire mist like the blue bloom of grapes.
Nearby a scarlet creeper trails a fence,
Nearer a hawthorn tree
Drops its wee crimson apples into the lush green grass.
I stand with head thrown back,
Seeing and breathing deep,
My arms stretched out, in my two hands
I hold a golden bowl.
Luscious fruits fulfil the yellow lustre of its hollow sphere,
Fruits like great gems,
A pear of russet topaz, a ruby peach,
A cluster of grapes--
Amethysts from the dewy cave of night--
A sapphire plum, a garnet apple, emerald nectarine,
And on them lies a rose.

Oh, empty golden bowl I call my soul,
Filled now with the precious fruits of life and time,
Topped with the rosy spray of grace,
A rose,
As though dropped to me from the sky above,
A crowning thing,
Love,
I lift and hold you out,
An offering,
And close my eyes.

The Autumn Rose
Antoinette de Coursey Patterson

A Ghostly visitant, pale Autumn Rose,
Haunting my garden that you once loved well:
Ah, how you queened it ere the sweet June's close,
And blushed anew to hear the zephyrs tell
Your loveliness was fairer than a dream!
But now your pride of beauty is all gone,
And like some poor sad penitent you seem,
Whose drooping head but hides a visage wan
And wasted by the coldness of the world.
Upon your faint sweet breath is borne a sigh,
Within your petals lies a tear impearled;
I hear you to my garden say good-bye.

A sudden wind--the pale rose-petals blow
Hither and yon--or are they flakes of snow?

A Carol of Harvest for 1867
Walt Whitman (first published in *The Galaxy*, 1867,
then in the 1872 edition of *Leaves of Grass*, with revisions,
as "The Return of Heroes")

1

A song of the grass and fields!
A song of the soil, and the good green grass!
A song no more of the city streets;
A song of the soil of the fields.

A song with the smell of sun-dried hay, where the nimble pitchers
handle the pitch-fork;

A song tasting of new wheat, and of fresh-husk'd maize.

2

For the lands, and for these passionate days, and for myself,
Now I awhile return to thee, O soil of Autumn fields,
Reclining on thy breast, giving myself to thee,
Answering the pulses of thy sane and equable heart,
Tuning a verse for thee.

O Earth, that hast no voice, confide to me a voice!
O harvest of my lands! O boundless Summer growths!
O lavish, brown, parturient earth! O infinite, teeming womb!
O theatre of time, and day, and night!
A verse, to seek to see, to narrate thee.

3

For still upon this stage,
I acted God's calm, annual drama;
Gorgeous processions, songs of birds,
Sunrise, that fullest feeds and freshens most the soul,
The heaving sea, the waves upon the shore, the musical, strong
waves,
The woods, the stalwart trees, the slender, tapering trees,
The flowers, the grass, the lilliput, countless armies of the grass,
The heat, the showers, the measureless pasturages,
The scenery of the snows, the wind's free orchestra,
The stretching, light-hung roof of clouds, the clear cerulean, and
the bulging, silvery fringes,
The high dilating stars, the placid, beckoning stars,
The shows of all the varied soils, and all the growths and products,
The moving flocks and herds, the plains and emerald meadows,
These for all ages', races' witnessing.

4

Fecund America! To-day,
Thou art all over set in births and joys!
Thou groan'st with riches! thy wealth clothes thee as with a swath-
ing garment!
Thou laughest loud with ache of great possessions!
A myriad-twining life, like interlacing vines, binds all thy vast de-
mesne!
As some huge ship, freighted to water's edge, thou ridest into port!
As rain falls from the heaven, and vapors rise from the earth, so
have the precious values fallen upon thee, and risen out of thee!
Thou envy of the globe! thou miracle!
Thou, bathed, choked, swimming in plenty!
Thou lucky Mistress of the tranquil barns!
Thou Prairie Dame that sittest in the middle, and lookest out upon
thy world, and lookest East, and lookest West!
Dispensatress, that by a word givest a thousand miles—that giv'st
a million farms, and missest nothing!
Thou All-Acceptress—thou Hospitable—(thou only art hospitable,
as God is hospitable.)

5

When last I sang, sad was my voice;
Sad were the shows around me, with deafening noises of hatred,
and smoke of conflict;
In the midst of the armies, the Heroes, I stood,
Or pass'd with slow step through the wounded and dying.

But now I sing not War,
Nor the measur'd march of soldiers, nor the tents of camps,
Nor the regiments hastily coming up, deploying in line of battle.

No more the dead and wounded;

No more the sad, unnatural shows of War.

Ask'd room those flush'd immortal ranks? the first forth-stepping armies?
Ask room, alas, the ghastly ranks—the armies dread that follow'd.

6

Pass—pass, ye proud brigades!
So handsome, dress'd in blue—with your tramping, sinewy legs;
With your shoulders young and strong—with your knapsacks and your muskets;
(How elate I stood and watch'd you, where, starting off, you march'd!)

Pass;—then rattle, drums, again!
Scream, you steamers on the river, out of whistles loud and shrill, your salutes!
For an army heaves in sight—O another gathering army!
Swarming, trailing on the rear—O you dread, accruing army!
O you regiments so piteous, with your mortal diarrhoea! with your fever!
O my land's maimed darlings! with the plenteous bloody bandage and the crutch!
Lo! your pallid army follow'd!

7

But on these days of brightness,
On the far-stretching beauteous landscape, the roads and lanes, the high-piled farm-wagons, and the fruits and barns,
Shall the dead intrude?

Yet the dead mar not—they also fit well in Nature;
They fit very well in the landscape, under the trees and grass,

And along the edge of the sky, in the horizon's far margin.

Nor do I forget you, departed;
Nor in Winter or Summer, my lost ones;
But most, in the open air, as now, when my soul is rapt and at
peace—like pleasing phantoms,
Your dear memories, rising, glide silently by me.

8

I saw the return of the Heroes;
(Yet the heroes never surpass'd, shall never return;
Them, that day, I saw not.)

I saw the great corps,
I saw them approaching, defiling by, with divisions,
Each, at its head, in the midst of his staff, the General.

I saw the processions of armies,
Streaming northward, their work done, they paused awhile in
clusters of mighty camps.

No holiday soldiers!—youthful, yet veterans;
Worn, swart, handsome, strong, of the stock of homestead and
workshop,
Harden'd of many a long campaign and sweaty march,
Inured on many a hard-fought, bloody field.

9

A pause—the armies wait;
A million flush'd, embattled conquerors wait;
The world, too, waits—then, soft as breaking night, and sure as
dawn,
They melt—they disappear.

Exult, indeed, O lands! victorious lands!
Not there your victory, on those red, shuddering fields;
But here and hence your victory.

Melt, melt away, ye armies! disperse, ye blue-clad soldiers!
Resolve ye back again—give up, for good, your deadly arms;
Other the arms, the fields henceforth for you, or South or North, or
East or West,
With saner wars—sweet wars—life-giving wars.

10

Loud, O my throat, and clear, O soul!
The season of thanks, and the voice of the carol of full-yielding;
The chant of joy and power for boundless fertility.

All till'd and untill'd fields expand before me;
I see the true arenas of my race and land—or first, or last,
Man's innocent and strong arenas.

I see the Heroes at other toils;
I see, well-wielded in their hands, the better weapons.

11

I see where America, Mother of All,
Well-pleased, with full-spanning eye, gazes forth, dwells long,
And counts the varied gathering of the products.

Busy the far, the sunlit panorama;
The western fields appear, with endless, prodigal surface;
(The steam-ploughs and horse-ploughs did their work well, and
the rotary spader did its work well.)

Lo! prairie, orchard, and the yellow grain of the North,
Cotton and rice of the South, and Louisiana cane;
Open, unseeded fallows, rich fields of clover and timothy,
Kine and horses feeding, and droves of sheep and swine,
And many a stately river flowing, and many a jocund brook,
And healthy uplands with their herby-perfumed breezes,
And the good green grass—that delicate miracle, the ever-
recurring grass.

12

Toil on, Heroes! harvest the products!
Not alone on those warlike fields, the Mother of All,
With dilated form and lambent eyes, watch'd you.

Toil on, Heroes! toil well! Handle the weapons well!
The Mother of All—yet here, as ever, she watches you.

13

Well-pleased, America, thou beholdest,
Over the fields of the West, those crawling monsters,
The human-divine inventions, the labor-saving implements:
Beholdest, moving in every direction, imbued as with life, the re-
volving hay-rakes,
The steam-power reaping-machines, and the horse-power ma-
chines,
The engines, thrashers of grain, and cleaners of grain, well separat-
ing the straw,
The power-hoes for corn-fields—the nimble work of the patent
pitch-fork;
Beholdest the newer saw-mill, the cotton-gin, and the rice-cleanser.

Beneath thy look, O Maternal,
With these, and else, and with their own strong hands, the Heroes

harvest.

All gather, and all harvest;
(Yet but for thee, O Powerful! not a scythe might swing, as now, in security;
Not a maize-stalk dangle, as now, its silken tassels in peace.)

14

Under Thee only they harvest—even but a wisp of hay, under thy great face, only;
Harvest the wheat of Ohio, Illinois, Wisconsin—every barbed spear, under thee;
Harvest the maize of Missouri, Kentucky, Tennessee—each ear in its light-green sheath,
Gather the hay to its myriad mows, in the odorous, tranquil barns,
Oats to their bins—the white potato, the buckwheat of Michigan, to theirs;
Gather the cotton in Mississippi or Alabama—dig and hoard the golden, the sweet potato of Georgia and the Carolinas,
Clip the wool of California or Pennsylvania,
Cut the flax in the Middle States, or hemp, or tobacco in the Borders,
Pick the pea and the bean, or pull apples from the trees, or bunches of grapes from the vines,
Or aught that ripens in all These States, or North or South,
Under the beaming sun, and under Thee.

Autumn Song
Dante Gabriel Rossetti

Know'st thou not at the fall of the leaf
How the heart feels a languid grief
Laid on it for a covering,
And how sleep seems a goodly thing
In Autumn at the fall of the leaf?

And how the swift beat of the brain
Falters because it is in vain,
In Autumn at the fall of the leaf
Knowest thou not? and how the chief
Of joys seems—not to suffer pain?

Know'st thou not at the fall of the leaf
How the soul feels like a dried sheaf
Bound up at length for harvesting,
And how death seems a comely thing
In Autumn at the fall of the leaf?

Autumn Fires

Robert Louis Stevenson (from *A Child's Garden of Verses*, 1885)

In the other gardens
And all up the vale,
From the autumn bonfires
See the smoke trail!

Pleasant summer over
And all the summer flowers,
The red fire blazes,
The gray smoke towers.

Sing a song of seasons!

Something bright in all!
Flowers in the summer,
Fires in the fall!

Indian Summer

Sara Teasdale

Lyric night of the lingering Indian Summer,
Shadowy fields that are scentless but full of singing,
Never a bird, but the passionless chant of insects,
  Ceaseless, insistent.

The grasshopper's horn, and far off, high in the maples
The wheel of a locust leisurely grinding the silence,
Under the moon waning and worn and broken,
  Tired with summer.

Let me remember you, voices of little insects,
Weeds in the moonlight, fields that are tangled with asters,
Let me remember you, soon will the winter be on us,
  Snow-hushed and heartless.

Over my soul murmur your mute benediction,
While I gaze, oh fields that rest after harvest,
As those who part look long in the eyes they lean to,
  Lest they forget them.

Merry Autumn

by Paul Laurence Dunbar

It's all a farce,—these tales they tell
About the breezes sighing,

And moans astir o'er field and dell,
Because the year is dying.

Such principles are most absurd,—
I care not who first taught 'em;
There's nothing known to beast or bird
To make a solemn autumn.

In solemn times, when grief holds sway
With countenance distressing,
You'll note the more of black and gray
Will then be used in dressing.

Now purple tints are all around;
The sky is blue and mellow;
And e'en the grasses turn the ground
From modest green to yellow.

The seed burs all with laughter crack
On featherweed and jimson;
And leaves that should be dressed in black
Are all decked out in crimson.

A butterfly goes winging by;
A singing bird comes after;
And Nature, all from earth to sky,
Is bubbling o'er with laughter.

The ripples wimple on the rills,
Like sparkling little lasses;
The sunlight runs along the hills,
And laughs among the grasses.

The earth is just so full of fun

It really can't contain it;
And streams of mirth so freely run
The heavens seem to rain it.

Don't talk to me of solemn days
In autumn's time of splendor,
Because the sun shows fewer rays,
And these grow slant and slender.

Why, it's the climax of the year,—
The highest time of living!—
Till naturally its bursting cheer
Just melts into thanksgiving.

"FROST TO-NIGHT"

Edith M. Thomas

Apple-green west and an orange bar,
And the crystal eye of a lone, one star ...
And, "Child, take the shears and cut what you will.
Frost to-night--so clear and dead-still."

Then, I sally forth, half sad, half proud,
And I come to the velvet, imperial crowd,
The wine-red, the gold, the crimson, the pied,--
The dahlias that reign by the garden-side.

The dahlias I might not touch till to-night!
A gleam of the shears in the fading light,
And I gathered them all,--the splendid throng,
And in one great sheaf I bore them along.

In my garden of Life with its all-late flowers
I heed a Voice in the shrinking hours:
"Frost to-night--so clear and dead-still ..."
Half sad, half proud, my arms I fill.

November Night

Adelaide Crapsey

Listen ...
With faint dry sound,
Like steps of passing ghosts,
The leaves, frost-crisp'd, break from the trees
And fall.

Poems of Winter

Sonnet 97

William Shakespeare

How like a winter hath my absence been
From thee, the pleasure of the fleeting year!
What freezings have I felt, what dark days seen!
What old December's bareness every where!
And yet this time removed was summer's time,
The teeming autumn, big with rich increase,
Bearing the wanton burden of the prime,
Like widow'd wombs after their lords' decease:
Yet this abundant issue seem'd to me
But hope of orphans and unfather'd fruit;
For summer and his pleasures wait on thee,
And, thou away, the very birds are mute;
Or, if they sing, 'tis with so dull a cheer
That leaves look pale, dreading the winter's near.

Now Winter Nights Enlarge

Thomas Campion

Now winter nights enlarge
The number of their hours,
And clouds their storms discharge
Upon the airy towers.
Let now the chimneys blaze,
And cups o'erflow with wine;
Let well-tuned words amaze
With harmony divine.
Now yellow waxen lights
Shall wait on honey love,
While youthful revels, masques, and courtly sights
Sleep's leaden spells remove.

This time doth well dispense
With lovers' long discourse;
Much speech hath some defence,
Though beauty no remorse.
All do not all things well;
Some measures comely tread,
Some knotted riddles tell,
Some poems smoothly read.
The summer hath his joys
And winter his delights;
Though love and all his pleasures are but toys,
They shorten tedious nights.

Sounds of the Winter
Walt Whitman

Sounds of the winter too,
Sunshine upon the mountains--many a distant strain
From cheery railroad train--from nearer field, barn, house,
The whispering air--even the mute crops, garner'd apples, corn,
Children's and women's tones--rhythm of many a farmer and of
flail,
An old man's garrulous lips among the rest, Think not we give out
yet,
Forth from these snowy hairs we keep up yet the lilt.

The Snow Gardens
Zoë Akins

  Like an empty stage
  The gardens are empty and cold;

The marble terraces rise
Like vases that hold no flowers;
The lake is frozen, the fountain still;
The marble walls and the seats
Are useless and beautiful.
Ah, here
Where the wind and the dusk and the snow are
All is silent and white and sad!
Why do I think of you?
Why does your name remorselessly
Strike through my heart?
Why does my soul awaken and shudder?
Why do I seem to hear
Cries as lovely as music?
Surely you never came
Into these pale snow-gardens;
Surely you never stood
Here in the twilight with me;
Yet here I have lingered and dreamed
Of a face as subtle as music,
Of golden hair, and of eyes
Like a child's ...
I have felt on my brow
Your finger-tips, plaintive as music ...
O Wonder of all wonders, O Love--
Wrought of sweet sounds and of dreaming!--
Why do you not emerge
From the lilac pale petals of dusk,
And come to me here in the gardens
Where the wind and the snow are?

Beauty and Peace are here--
And unceasing music--
And a loneliness chill and wistful,
Like the feeling of death.

Like a crystal lily a star
Leans from its leaves of silver
And gleams in the sky;
And golden and faint in the shadows
You wait indistinctly,--
Like a phantom lamp that appears
In the mirror of distance that hovers
By the window at twilight--
You have come--and we stand together,
With questioning eyes--
Dreaming and cold and ghostly
In an empty garden that seems
Like an empty stage.

Winter: A Dirge
Robert Burns

The wintry west extends his blast,
And hail and rain does blaw;
Or the stormy north sends driving forth
The blinding sleet and snaw:
While, tumbling brown, the burn comes down,
And roars frae bank to brae;
And bird and beast in covert rest,
And pass the heartless day.

"The sweeping blast, the sky o'ercast,"
The joyless winter day
Let others fear, to me more dear
Than all the pride of May:
The tempest's howl, it soothes my soul,
My griefs it seems to join;
The leafless trees my fancy please,

Their fate resembles mine!

Thou Power Supreme, whose mighty scheme
These woes of mine fulfil,
Here firm I rest; they must be best,
Because they are *Thy* will!
Then all I want—O do Thou grant
This one request of mine!—
Since to *enjoy* Thou dost deny,
Assist me to *resign.*

To Winter

William Blake (from *Poetical Sketches*, 1783)

O winter! bar thine adamantine doors:
The north is thine; there hast thou built thy dark
Deep-founded habitation. Shake not thy roofs
Nor bend thy pillars with thine iron car.

He hears me not, but o'er the yawning deep
Rides heavy; his storms are unchain'd, sheathed
In ribbed steel; I dare not lift mine eyes;
For he hath rear'd his sceptre o'er the world.

Lo! now the direful monster, whose skin clings
To his strong bones, strides o'er the groaning rocks:
He withers all in silence, and in his hand
Unclothes the earth, and freezes up frail life.

He takes his seat upon the cliffs, the mariner
Cries in vain. Poor little wretch! that deal'st
With storms, till heaven smiles, and the monster
Is driven yelling to his caves beneath Mount Hecla.

A Song For Winter

Mrs. Schyler Van Rensselaer

Speak not of snow and cold and rime
  Now they prevail.
Would you have joy in winter-time,
  Think of the pale
New green that comes, of blossoming lilacs think,
Larkspur, and borders of the fringèd pink.
And sing, if winter grants you heart to sing,
  Of summer and of spring.

Would you secure some happiness
  In frosty hours,
Trust to the eye external less
  Than to the powers
Of inward sight that even now may show
Opaline seas, blue hilltops, and the glow
Of daybreak on the glades where thrushes sing
  In summer and in spring.

Gaze not on fettered lake and brook
  And sullen skies,
But in your happy memory look
  Where beauty lies
As once it was, as it shall be again
When sunshine floods the fields of blowing grain,
And sing, as must who would in winter sing,
  Of summer and of spring.

Frost at Midnight

Samuel Taylor Coleridge

The Frost performs its secret ministry,
Unhelped by any wind. The owlet's cry
Came loud--and hark, again! loud as before.
The inmates of my cottage, all at rest,
Have left me to that solitude, which suits
Abstruser musings: save that at my side
My cradled infant slumbers peacefully.
'Tis calm indeed! so calm, that it disturbs
And vexes meditation with its strange
And extreme silentness. Sea, hill, and wood,
This populous village! Sea, and hill, and wood,
With all the numberless goings-on of life,
Inaudible as dreams! the thin blue flame
Lies on my low-burnt fire, and quivers not;
Only that film, which fluttered on the grate,
Still flutters there, the sole unquiet thing.
Methinks, its motion in this hush of nature
Gives it dim sympathies with me who live,
Making it a companionable form,
Whose puny flaps and freaks the idling Spirit
By its own moods interprets, every where
Echo or mirror seeking of itself,
And makes a toy of Thought.

But O! how oft,
How oft, at school, with most believing mind,
Presageful, have I gazed upon the bars,
To watch that fluttering stranger! and as oft
With unclosed lids, already had I dreamt
Of my sweet birth-place, and the old church-tower,
Whose bells, the poor man's only music, rang
From morn to evening, all the hot Fair-day,

So sweetly, that they stirred and haunted me
With a wild pleasure, falling on mine ear
Most like articulate sounds of things to come!
So gazed I, till the soothing things, I dreamt,
Lulled me to sleep, and sleep prolonged my dreams!
And so I brooded all the following morn,
Awed by the stern preceptor's face, mine eye
Fixed with mock study on my swimming book:
Save if the door half opened, and I snatched
A hasty glance, and still my heart leaped up,
For still I hoped to see the *stranger's* face,
Townsman, or aunt, or sister more beloved,
My play-mate when we both were clothed alike!

Dear Babe, that sleepest cradled by my side,
Whose gentle breathings, heard in this deep calm,
Fill up the interspersèd vacancies
And momentary pauses of the thought!
My babe so beautiful! it thrills my heart
With tender gladness, thus to look at thee,
And think that thou shalt learn far other lore,
And in far other scenes! For I was reared
In the great city, pent 'mid cloisters dim,
And saw nought lovely but the sky and stars.
But thou, my babe! shalt wander like a breeze
By lakes and sandy shores, beneath the crags
Of ancient mountain, and beneath the clouds,
Which image in their bulk both lakes and shores
And mountain crags: so shalt thou see and hear
The lovely shapes and sounds intelligible
Of that eternal language, which thy God
Utters, who from eternity doth teach
Himself in all, and all things in himself.
Great universal Teacher! he shall mould
Thy spirit, and by giving make it ask.

Therefore all seasons shall be sweet to thee,
Whether the summer clothe the general earth
With greenness, or the redbreast sit and sing
Betwixt the tufts of snow on the bare branch
Of mossy apple-tree, while the nigh thatch
Smokes in the sun-thaw; whether the eave-drops fall
Heard only in the trances of the blast,
Or if the secret ministry of frost
Shall hang them up in silent icicles,
Quietly shining to the quiet Moon.

In drear-nighted December

John Keats

In drear-nighted December,
Too happy, happy tree,
Thy branches ne'er remember
Their green felicity:
The north cannot undo them
With a sleety whistle through them;
Nor frozen thawings glue them
From budding at the prime.

In drear-nighted December,
Too happy, happy brook,
Thy bubblings ne'er remember
Apollo's summer look;
But with a sweet forgetting,
They stay their crystal fretting,
Never, never petting
About the frozen time.

Ah! would 'twere so with many

A gentle girl and boy!
But were there ever any
Writhed not at passed joy?
The feel of not to feel it,
When there is none to heal it
Nor numbed sense to steel it,
Was never said in rhyme.

Winter Stores

Charlotte Brontë (published under her *nom de plume*, Currer Bell in 1846)

We take from life one little share,
And say that this shall be
A space, redeemed from toil and care,
From tears and sadness free.

And, haply, Death unstrings his bow,
And Sorrow stands apart,
And, for a little while, we know
The sunshine of the heart.

Existence seems a summer eve,
Warm, soft, and full of peace,
Our free, unfettered feelings give
The soul its full release.

A moment, then, it takes the power
To call up thoughts that throw
Around that charmed and hallowed hour,
This life's divinest glow.

But Time, though viewlessly it flies,

And slowly, will not stay;
Alike, through clear and clouded skies,
It cleaves its silent way.

Alike the bitter cup of grief,
Alike the draught of bliss,
Its progress leaves but moment brief
For baffled lips to kiss

The sparkling draught is dried away,
The hour of rest is gone,
And urgent voices, round us, say,
"'Ho, lingerer, hasten on!"

And has the soul, then, only gained,
From this brief time of ease,
A moment's rest, when overstrained,
One hurried glimpse of peace?

No; while the sun shone kindly o'er us,
And flowers bloomed round our feet, —
While many a bud of joy before us
Unclosed its petals sweet, —

An unseen work within was plying;
Like honey-seeking bee,
From flower to flower, unwearied, flying,
Laboured one faculty, —

Thoughtful for Winter's future sorrow,
Its gloom and scarcity;
Prescient to-day, of want to-morrow,
Toiled quiet Memory.

'Tis she that from each transient pleasure

Extracts a lasting good;
'Tis she that finds, in summer, treasure
To serve for winter's food.

And when Youth's summer day is vanished,
And Age brings Winter's stress,
Her stores, with hoarded sweets replenished,
Life's evening hours will bless.

Winter-Time

Robert Louis Stevenson (from *A Child's Garden of Verses*, 1885)

Late lies the wintry sun a-bed,
A frosty, fiery sleepy-head;
Blinks but an hour or two; and then,
A blood-red orange, sets again.

Before the stars have left the skies,
At morning in the dark I rise;
And shivering in my nakedness,
By the cold candle, bathe and dress.

Close by the jolly fire I sit
To warm my frozen bones a bit;
Or with a reindeer-sled, explore
The colder countries round the door.

When to go out, my nurse doth wrap
Me in my comforter and cap;
The cold wind burns my face, and blows
Its frosty pepper up my nose.

Black are my steps on silver sod;

Thick blows my frosty breath abroad;
And tree and house, and hill and lake,
Are frosted like a wedding-cake.

Winter Heavens
George Meredith

Sharp is the night, but stars with frost alive
Leap off the rim of earth across the dome.
It is a night to make the heavens our home
More than the nest whereto apace we strive.
Lengths down our road each fir-tree seems a hive,
In swarms outrushing from the golden comb.
They waken waves of thoughts that burst to foam:
The living throb in me, the dead revive.
Yon mantle clothes us: there, past mortal breath,
Life glistens on the river of the death.
It folds us, flesh and dust; and have we knelt,
Or never knelt, or eyed as kine the springs
Of radiance, the radiance enrings:
And this is the soul's haven to have felt.

London Snow
Robert Bridges

When men were all asleep the snow came flying,
In large white flakes falling on the city brown,
Stealthily and perpetually settling and loosely lying,
Hushing the latest traffic of the drowsy town;
Deadening, muffling, stifling its murmurs failing;
Lazily and incessantly floating down and down:

The Sugar Maple Press Anthology of Nature Poems

Silently sifting and veiling road, roof and railing;
Hiding difference, making unevenness even,
Into angles and crevices softly drifting and sailing.
All night it fell, and when full inches seven
It lay in the depth of its uncompacted lightness,
The clouds blew off from a high and frosty heaven;
And all woke earlier for the unaccustomed brightness
Of the winter dawning, the strange unheavenly glare:
The eye marvelled — marvelled at the dazzling whiteness;
The ear hearkened to the stillness of the solemn air;
No sound of wheel rumbling nor of foot falling,
And the busy morning cries came thin and spare.
Then boys I heard, as they went to school, calling,
They gathered up the crystal manna to freeze
Their tongues with tasting, their hands with snowballing;
Or rioted in a drift, plunging up to the knees;
Or peering up from under the white-mossed wonder,
'O look at the trees!' they cried, 'O look at the trees!'
With lessened load a few carts creak and blunder,
Following along the white deserted way,
A country company long dispersed asunder:
When now already the sun, in pale display
Standing by Paul's high dome, spread forth below
His sparkling beams, and awoke the stir of the day.
For now doors open, and war is waged with the snow;
And trains of sombre men, past tale of number,
Tread long brown paths, as toward their toil they go:
But even for them awhile no cares encumber
Their minds diverted; the daily word is unspoken,
The daily thoughts of labour and sorrow slumber
At the sight of the beauty that greets them, for the charm they have
broken.

Winter in Durnover Field

Thomas Hardy

Scene.—A wide stretch of fallow ground recently sown with
wheat,
and frozen to iron hardness. Three large birds walking about
thereon,
and wistfully eyeing the surface. Wind keen from north-east: sky a
dull grey.

(Triolet)

Rook.—Throughout the field I find no grain;
The cruel frost encrusts the cornland!
Starling.—Aye: patient pecking now is vain
Throughout the field, I find...
Rook.—No grain!
Pigeon.—Nor will be, comrade, till it rain,
Or genial thawings loose the lorn land
Throughout the field.
Rook.—I find no grain:
The cruel frost encrusts the cornland!

Day After the Snowstorm

Greg Fox

Ice blue sky
Powdered sugar breeze
Whipped cream woods

Soon Shall the Winter's Foil Be Here

Walt Whitman

Soon shall the winter's foil be here;
Soon shall these icy ligatures unbind and melt.
A little while,
And air, soil, wave, suffused shall be in softness,
bloom and growth; a thousand forms
shall rise
From these dead clods and chills as from low
burial graves.
Thine eyes, ears—all thy best attributes—all
that takes cognizance of natural beauty—
Shall wake and fill. Thou shalt perceive the
simple shows, delicate miracles of earth,
Dandelions, clover, the emerald grass, the early
scents and flowers,
The arbutus under foot, the willow's yellow-
green, the blossoming plum and cherry;
With these the robin, lark and thrush singing
their songs—the flitting bluebird;
For such the scenes the annual endless play
brings on.

The Sugar Maple Press Anthology of Nature Poems

Index of Poets

A note about the photos …. I took all of the photos in this book in Vermont and on Long Island, New York, (and one of them in California. I'll let you guess which one was taken in California... I don't think it will be too hard to figure out!)

—Greg Fox

Environmental Links

I wanted to include a list of helpful links for anyone interested in getting involved in helping to save the environment. Instead, I discovered one website which seems to cover all the bases:

www.world.org

This website has a huge database of links to various websites covering a wide variety of environmental topics including preservation of natural habitats, organic farming, endangered species preservation, nutritional treatments for health conditions, renewable energy, the reduction of fossil fuel consumption, climate change, animal rescue, and other related environmental topics. So, if you're at all interested in such topics, this is a good place to start.

Greg Fox is the writer/illustrator of the nationally syndicated comic strip "Kyle's Bed & Breakfast". He received a B.A. from Geneseo College in up-state New York. This is the first collection of poetry he has ever compiled. He currently resides in Northport, Long Island, New York. His work can be viewed online at:

www.kylecomics.com

Thank You!

www.ingramcontent.com/pod-product-compliance
Lightning Source LLC
Chambersburg PA
CBHW022013090426
42741CB00007B/1020